A Land Called
California

A Land Called
California

J. Robert Dean

Pacific Sun Press
Del Mar, California 92014

Library of Congress Catalog Card No.: 79-88662
ISBN: 0-9602908-1-8
Printed in the United States of America.
10 9 8 7 6 5 4 3 2 1

Editor: Linda Wood
Designer: Louie Neiheisel
Illustration: Louie Neiheisel and Kitty Anderson
Assistant Designer and Art production: Cher Threinen
Typography: Thompson Type, San Diego, California
Printed by: Graphic Arts Center, Portland, Oregon

iv

I would like to dedicate this book to
my father for his inspiration and to
my wife, Donna, for her continuing support.

Contents

*Photographs only

The Northeast Volcanic Region

Wildly fascinating and romantic country, the Northeast Volcanic Region is a vast, rough lava plain broken by volcanic peaks and dissected by streams, offering a striking contrast to the low desert plain which lies to the south. A land of irregular lava rock, this area is the home of wild game, fish, and fowl and was once a bloody Native American battleground.

North of the Sierra Nevada lies the Cascade Mountain Range with its rugged, lofty peaks in the west and its lava flows in the east. Of the many volcanoes that crown its summit, Mount Shasta is the most spectacular, with its snowcapped cone which is a towering landmark throughout northeastern California. Within Lassen Volcanic National Park is the famous Lassen Peak, which still displays receding volcanic activity. Last active during 1915 and 1917, this volcano destroyed forests for miles around and left masses of pumice and volcanic ash on the ground. The area surrounding Lassen Peak makes up what is perhaps the largest lava field in the world. Extending eastward, an estimated quarter of a million square miles, it covers a large part of north-

ern California, Oregon, Washington, British Columbia, and Montana. Today Lassen Peak stands as the only glowing ember amidst a land of burned-out fires.

Millions of years ago, glaciers covered all of Mount Shasta as well as some of the other higher peaks of the Cascades. During the period of greatest activity, the glaciers descended the slopes of Mount Shasta, crossed the valley below, and rose to heights of 4,000 feet along the ridges to the west. The valley north of Mount Shasta was covered with ice that was 1,000 feet thick in places.

Today glaciers cover only about three square miles of Mount Shasta, with the Hotlum Glacier on the north side accounting for almost half of this area. As a result of low precipitation levels and higher summer temperatures, glaciers on Mount Shasta are now beginning to recede and no longer attain the same levels at which they were originally observed a century ago.

The landscape east of the Cascades is more subdued and the vegetation cover less dense. Lower precipitation levels and the porous quality of the underlying surface contribute to the

loss of soil moisture. A perfect example of this porous lava can be found in McArthur-Burney Falls where water issues out of the lava face of the waterfall.

Most of the surface features of the Modoc Plateau are relatively young, although older highland areas can be found in the southeastern parts of the province. These older upland areas were formed by volcanic deposits which were faulted and uplifted above the rest of the area. The lower areas were subsequently covered by volcanic flows.

Because lava flows in the province were highly liquid, they produced a thin rock surface which covered the underlying topography and formed an irregular plain. Then more viscous flows, which erupted from central vents, formed a series of broad low-shield volcanoes, cinder cones, and irregular flows of lava. These flows produced an unusual landscape characterized by great surface roughness and tunnels marking underground flows. As the volcanic cycle tapered off, the eruptions became localized and more explosive. What remains are chunks of rough rock material surrounded by almost perfectly preserved cinder cones.

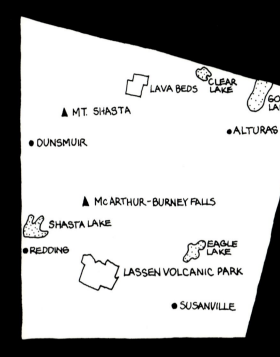

Lava Beds

It was almost as though the earth was angry. She wrenched and twisted the surface of northern California, and the sky was bright with explosions. Monstrous rivers of molten basaltic lava poured forth from underground fissures. Then, as the surface of the lava cooled, the still-molten core drained away leaving the lava tube caves that are visible today.

Lava Beds National Monument is in the northeast portion of California near the

Oregon border. It is a region of rugged, diverse wilderness where ancient lava flows, caves, black obsidian hills, cinder cones, and lava chimneys dominate the landscape. The monument contains some 293 caves, each with distinct floor, ceiling, and wall development. In Valentine Cave, one can see examples of rippled lava flow on its floor. Another, called Hopkins Chocolate Cave, was formed when hot gases above the lava remelted the ceiling, causing the lava to drip down the sides of the cavern like melting chocolate. Natural Bridge Cave is so named for the lava bridge that crosses its entrance. Most of the monument is covered with relatively smooth, pahoehoe (pah-hoy-hoy) lava; however, Devil's Homestead Flow and Schonchin Flow offer examples of rougher aa (ah-ah) flows.

Clearly among the most outstanding features of the Lava Beds are the seventeen cinder cones found in the monument. One of the largest of these, Schonchin Butte, was named after one of the Modoc Indian war chiefs in memory of the only major Native American war fought in California. The Modoc War, which occurred in 1872, was waged as an attempt by the Indians to resist the white man's efforts to place them on a reservation. As a result, the war was one of the most costly in military history in terms of expenditure of capital and human lives. It was the unique terrain of the stronghold in which the Modocs took refuge, as well as the Indians' knowledge of how to use that terrain to their advantage, that enabled them to stave off the enemy for six months before they fell to defeat.

Devil's Homestead Lava Flow in Lava Beds National Monument

*Native American paintings (pictographs) found in
Big Painted Cave and Symbol Bridge Cave*

Schonchin Butte is a 5,253-foot cinder cone named after a Modoc Indian chief.

*Skull Ice Cave. Notice
hiker holding lantern at lower right.*

Schonchin Lava Flow is an excellent example of the rough lava flows indigenous to this region.

View from the interior of Natural Bridge Cave

These unusual wall patterns are found on the interior of Hopkins Chocolate Cave.

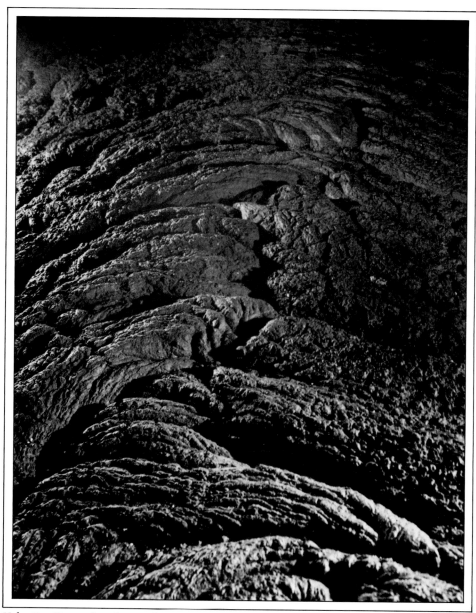

*Valentine Cave is best known for its
rippled, lava floor patterns.*

Mount Shasta

It is an inviting mountain, this great snow peak called Shasta, which on clear days can be seen from as many as 200 miles away. Many travelers consider Shasta to be the most magnificent of California's many mountains. Yet this great dormant volcano is not the state's loftiest peak. In fact, five higher summits can be found in the Sierra Nevada Range far to the south.

But for sheer, overwhelming size no mountain in California can rival Shasta, and few peaks in the world are bulkier. From an almost circular base with a diameter of some 17 miles, its majestic cone sweeps upward to an altitude of 14,160 feet and has a volume of some 80 cubic miles. Particularly remarkable is the fact that the mountain towers more than 5,000 feet above every surrounding

peak and ridge within a radius of 75 miles.

In relatively recent geological time an unusually active secondary vent opened up high on the western flank, causing the rapid formation of a steep subsidiary cone now called Shastina. This crater, which is 1.5 miles west of the main summit, rises to an elevation of 12,300 feet. Side by side, the two cones make Shasta a distinctive double-topped mountain.

It is not certain exactly when Shasta's volcanic activity ceased, but the steaming sulphur springs 200 feet below the highest point suggest that the subterranean fires are not completely extinguished. When on April 30, 1875, John Muir and a companion were trapped in a blizzard near the summit, they were forced to lie for thirteen hours in this same sulphur hot spring, being scalded on one side and nearly frozen on the other. Experts tell us that the mountain could erupt again at any time, as did Lassen Peak, which was last active in 1914.

Unlike many mountains of volcanic origin, which were formed by one vast upheaval, Shasta was built up gradually by successive eruptions of lava and ashes, interrupted by long periods of silence and inactivity, as is shown by the structure of sections cut by glacial action. Twice during the glacial period Mount Shasta was capped by a huge ice mantle which leveled and destroyed its crater and remodeled the entire mountain from summit to base. Today five small glaciers are still at work, putting the finishing touches on Shasta's steep upper slopes.

Southwest exposure of Mount Shasta

Lassen Volcanic Park

Wrought by flames, lava, and cinders, Lassen Volcanic National Park affords some of the most unusual natural phenomena found anywhere in California. Mount Lassen, which rises to an altitude of 10,500 feet, offers a majestic sight to the viewer, and even its fireblasted surroundings possess a weird natural beauty. The park also contains several smaller volcanic peaks, fantastic lava fields, both ancient and modern, fumaroles, hot springs, and mud volcanoes, as well as boiling lakes and other interesting spectacles indigenous to a volcanic region.

Bumpass Hell is a fascinating miniature Yellowstone Park, replete with rumbling steam vents, boiling mudpots, thermal springs, and encrusted ground surfaces. The sulphur works, at the south entrance to the park, display similar phenomena; and scores of hot springs, some not as big around as a dime, bubble

busily while caldrons of hot gray mud ooze and burble, and steaming water emerges from snow drifts.

Mount Lassen, which had lain dormant for many centuries, awakened again in 1914. On May 30th of that year came the first in a series of some 300 eruptions that continued to occur through 1917. The most dramatic performance, which took place on May 19, 1915, resulted when lava spilled over the northeastern rim, steam roared out of a hole near the top of the mountain, and large chunks of lava cascaded down the slopes. When heat from the volcanic fires melted the deep drifts of snow, the water, combined with the debris from earlier eruptions, created a devastating mudflow. The deluge of mud surged down the mountain, growing both in volume and violence, peeling the bark off trees for as high as eighteen feet, and submerging nearby meadows under as much as six feet of debris. And still Lassen Peak was not through. Three days later, a spectacular column of smoke mounted 40,000 feet into the sky and an explosion of steam and hot gases shot down the mountainside. This time the force of the steam jet was horizontal and the blast killed every living thing in its path and flattened trees for three miles. The northeast side of Lasen Peak was stripped of all vegetation, its earth scrubbed bare. As far away as Reno, Nevada, streets were buried under several inches of ash. After this huge blast, declining eruptions continued for a few years, but since then the grumbling old giant has remained asleep.

Lassen Peak

Bumpass Hell, named after George Bumpass who lost a leg here when he accidentally stepped into one of the area's many steaming pools.

Boiling mudpots

Icy Lake Helen as it appears in midsummer

White Bark Pines

Marmots like this one are found in Lassen Park and are known as "guardians of the trail."

Snow bend caused by heavy winter snows resting against the tree's trunk

Late afternoon reflection of Lassen Peak in Manzanita Lake.

Pinkish lava remains of landslides at Chaos Crags

McArthur-Burney Falls _____

McArthur-Burney Falls State Park is located in the beautiful evergreen forests of the Pit River country. The spectacular waterfall is certainly the main attraction within the park. But it is the park itself,

as well as the territory that surrounds it, that makes a visit to McArthur-Burney a memorable and satisfying experience. Located halfway between Mount Shasta and Lassen Peak, the park has barely changed since the days when the Hudson Bay Company fur hunters regularly passed through here on their way to and from California along the old Pit River Route.

Just inside the park, Burney Creek wells up out of its subterranean source and rushes toward Burney Falls. Just above the main cascade the creek hurries over a small preliminary fall. It then separates into a double cataract, divided by a rock island, and goes streaming over the main 129-foot-high cliff into an emerald-colored pool of water. On sunlit mornings a little rainbow can be seen in the mist that blows down the canyon from the foot of the falls.

But what makes Burney Falls uniquely captivating are the countless small streams of white water issuing out of the porous rock that form a curtain all across the cliff behind the two main streams of falling water. These small streams add considerably to the beauty of the falls and remind us of this region's fascinating volcanic history.

A great variety of birds can be seen in the park, but two species are of special interest. Black swifts can be recognized by their color, their pointed wings, and the quick, darting, seemingly erratic flight patterns they use as they pursue insects. Bald eagles also live in this region, and there are several active nests in the vicinity of the park.

McArthur-Burney Falls

The Sierra Nevada Mountain Region

Certain sights and places are so magnificent in their scope and yet so enchanting in their detail that they almost defy description. Too durable to be altered by the passage of time and too vast to be conquered by humans, they seem almost eternal.

The Sierra Nevada is a perfect example of such a place. It is a country of vast distances where whole mountainsides of untouched forests remain intact. There are flower-strewn meadows where deer roam undisturbed, miles of fishing streams, beautiful clear lakes, and the Sierra high country. On the steep eastern slope, the mountains rise two miles high while the gentler western slope, which is robed in forests, serves as a mountain playground.

This California mountain range is renowned throughout the world. Most foreign mountaineers can easily identify a picture of Yosemite Valley, with its unique vertical walls and its cascades plunging from suspended valleys. Nature lovers around the world are aware of the Sierra's spectacular Big Trees, which are the largest trees in the world and grow exclusively in this area. People with only limited knowledge of American history know about the famous Gold Rush to these mountains that began in 1849. Perhaps no other American mountain range has achieved as much literary fame as the Sierra Nevada, which has been immortalized in the tales of Bret Harte and Mark Twain and praised in the writings of John Muir, one of the most engaging naturalists of modern times.

Glaciers have sculptured the peaks, swept away the soil, bitten deeply into the rocks, enlarged stream channels, and polished the surface of the Sierra's bare mountains. Were it not for the rich, open forests on the western slope, the area would appear almost completely barren. Although glacial activity has been the primary agent in shaping the Sierra's surface features, today glaciers play only a minor role in the landscape. Those that do remain are small and cling precariously to shady cirques high up under the loftiest summits. Even Palisade Glacier, which is the largest, is only a mile and a half long. But despite its size it is remarkably impressive in its arctic setting of 14,000-foot peaks, and exhibits all the characteristics—glacier tables, crevasses, and moraines—of much larger glaciers.

The Sierra Nevada extends 430 miles from the Tehachapi Pass in the south to its northern limits a few miles south of Lassen Peak. It varies

in width from 40 to 80 miles. Geologists tell us that the entire range is made up of a single massive block of the earth's crust. It includes not only the 14,495-foot Mount Whitney, which is the highest peak outside Alaska, but several other peaks almost as high. It also contains Tahoe, the West's largest mountain lake. But even more important to Californians is the fact that the Sierra Nevada contains eight million acres of national forests, one and a half million acres of national parks, and many outstanding state parks.

In addition, the Sierra Nevada is California's weather factory as well as its major source of water. Its high-crested peaks force the moist air flowing off the ocean to rise, which in turn causes rain and snow to be released on the mountains. The snow pack, which is the nation's deepest (with a record of 72 feet), builds up through the winter as successive storms alternate with spells of bright, sunny weather. The warmth of the granite and the winter sun melt enough snow to keep the streams running throughout the winter. By late spring, the storms subside and the snow melts almost completely, swelling the rivers that provide water for much of the state of California.

Plumas-Eureka

High on the northern slopes of the Sierra Nevada, Plumas-Eureka State Park is cradled amid spectacular mountain scenery in the headwater country of the Feather River. Glacier-carved granite peaks rise high above the timberline to dominate the horizon while beautiful verdant forests cover the lower slopes.

Within the park, the historic mining town of Johnsville and the partially restored Plumas-Eureka stamp mill serve as vivid reminders of the days when hard-rock gold mining was the region's primary activity. The Gold Rush of 1849 had a profound effect on this relatively remote part of the Sierra Nevada. Throughout the 1850s, numerous placer claims were established and hard-rock mining was undertaken. Then in 1872, the Sierra Buttes Mining Company moved in and purchased most of the mines, consolidating the various uncoordinated activities of the earlier operators

and launching a highly efficient mining program that was to return handsome profits.

Under the direction of the company's local superintendent, William Johns, a new town was established and named Johnsville. Three tramways were built to transport ore down to a central mill near Johnsville, and the record shows that at one time there were as many as 400 workers in the company's mines and stamp mills.

After 1890, the mines began to taper off in productivity. As the years went by there were occasional periods of excitement in which renewed prosperity seemed always just around the corner, but little by little the mining operations dwindled until they were finally discontinued in 1943.

Today, both in and around the park, there are still many visible reminders of the area's colorful history. Not the least of these are the numerous sealed-off mine shafts and tunnels. And there is the partially restored stamp mill where some $80 million worth of gold is said to have been processed. The building that now houses the park headquarters and museum originally served as a bunkhouse for one of the mines.

Also standing is part of an old mine tramway that is said to have been the world's first ski lift. In fact, it may well be that the early miners who wintered in Plumas-Eureka were the first Americans to organize, advertise, and wager on highly competitive downhill (Alpine) ski races, using what were then called "snowshoes" or "long boards."

Plumas-Eureka Stamp Mill, where millions
of dollars' worth of ore was refined

The forested valley of Plumas-Eureka Park

Johnsville as it appears today

Lake Tahoe

In *Roughing It*, Mark Twain gave us a memorable description of Lake Tahoe: "We plodded on, and at last the lake burst upon us, a noble sheet of blue water . . . walled in by a rim of snow-clad peaks that towered aloft full 3,000 feet higher still. As it lay there with the shadows of the mountains brilliantly photographed upon its still surface, I thought it must surely be the fairest picture the whole earth affords."

Settled high in the Sierra Nevada amidst a lofty region of beauty, Lake Tahoe is indeed one of the world's grandest mountain lakes. Its immense depth, clarity of water, intensity of color, size, and above all, its setting among crested mountain peaks makes it truly distinctive.

One of the largest and highest mountain lakes in existence, Lake Tahoe is a mile high, approximately 21 miles long, and 12 miles wide. It is fringed by a series of mountain peaks, snow-clad except for a few brief weeks in summer, which tower to heights of 9,000 to 12,000 feet. Its shores are rimmed with forests of huge fir, spruce, and tamarack pines.

Lake Tahoe is cradled between the rugged, glaciated crest of the Sierra Nevada on the west and the more subdued divide of the Carson Range on the east. What we see today is the end product of a series of geological processes that began many millions of years ago. First came the mountain building which raised the Sierra Nevada. Then the area was subjected to a period of violent volcanic action during which great masses of lava were spread over the region and a natural dam was formed. This was followed by a period of glaciation which completed the natural dam that today holds Lake Tahoe. Time and erosion added the final touches to this unique mountain lake.

To many, the main charm of Lake Tahoe is the exquisite, rare, and astonishing color of its water. Brilliant blues, vivid greens, and delicate shadings of purple, violet, and cobalt may be seen in the crystal purity of the lake's waters. Many of the softer color effects are produced by the light-colored sands that are washed down into the shallower waters by mountain streams. These vary from white and cream to deep yellow, brown, and red.

Tahoe's waters strongly reflect the moods of the weather and the season of the year. Following sunset on crisp autumn evenings scarlet and orange hues spread over the water. At sunrise striking yellows and golds fan out across the lake and gradually turn into the deep blue of the Sierra morning sky. However, when clouds block out the sun and drift across the lake its surface changes to a mirror of silver gray.

Winter at Lake Tahoe's Emerald Bay

Lake Tahoe, one of the highest and largest mountain lakes in the world

Mono Craters and Mono Lake___

Mono Craters are a remarkable chain of extinct volcanoes extending south from Mono Lake along the eastern foot of the Sierra Nevada. This prehistoric land of pumice and obsidian is a unique combination of unusual geological exhibits and fine scenery.

The craters are a series of obsidian domes rising from a hilly plain. They are composed of obsidian (or volcanic glass) and pumice, a stone so light that it will float on water. Visitors are always astonished to discover how easily they can lift these huge pumice rocks.

The gray, steep-sloped cones, 20 in all, rise to 3,000 feet above the surrounding 6,500-foot plain. The craters, most of which are still unnamed, were formed by a series of volcanic eruptions. During their formation, molten obsidian rose in the center of the craters. The obsidian cooled rapidly and the hard, brittle, natural glass cracked and fractured as it overflowed from the volcanic cones. Local Native Americans fashioned the stony glass fragments into razor-sharp arrowheads.

Mono Lake appears sparkling and fresh, but it is actually a briny deep in which only one small species of saltwater shrimp and the larvae of black flies can live. Its water is so impregnated with alkaline materials that heavy storms leave a soapy foam along its shore several feet thick. The lake achieved literary notoriety in Mark Twain's *Roughing It* in which Twain tells the story of how a dog achieved a running record of 250 miles an hour after taking a swim in the lake.

This miniature Dead Sea has two small islands, Paoha and Negit, that serve as a rookery for thousands of sea gulls from the San Francisco Bay region. Each spring the gulls wing their way across the Sierra Nevada to lay their eggs on the lava rocks of these islands. Here they raise their young and feed on the brine shrimp in the lake.

John Fremont, Joseph Walker, and Kit Carson were among the early pioneers who passed through this country. In fact, one of Kit Carson's daughters is said to be buried at the edge of Mono Lake beneath some cottonwoods. Later, gold miners came to the area and established mines and small towns. The region became so prosperous that in 1879 a steamship, the U.S.S. Rocket, was hauled from Carson City, Nevada, by mule teams to operate on the lake. Cordwood and lumber were cut and shipped across Mono Lake and taken to Bodie and other mining towns in the area.

Mono Craters

An impending thunderstorm threatens Mono Lake.

Bodie

"Goodby, God! I'm moving to Bodie," was the prayerful farewell of one young girl whose family was preparing to leave for "the wickedest town of the West." The Reverend F. M. Warrington described it in 1881 as "a sea of sin lashed by the tempests of lust and passion." Bodie claimed the largest Chinatown in the West outside of San Francisco. The same claim was made for its red-light district whose two main streets were known as "Maiden Lane" and "Virgin Alley." Among the inhabitants of the district were such legendary "ladies of the evening" as Rosa Mae of the Highgrade, Emma Goldsmith of the Ozark, Beautiful Doll, and Madame Moustache.

In 1878 the town grew in population from 20 to 10,000 and boasted of having the "wickedest men, the wildest streets, and the worst climate out-of-doors." Murder was commonplace and occurred at the slightest provocation and with startling regularity, an average of once a day. Robberies, stagecoach holdups, and street fights provided some variety.

A cold-blooded murder took place after a New Year's dance when "Frenchy" De Roche persisted in dancing with Mrs. Treloar over the objections of her husband, Tom Treloar. As Tom was leaving the dance, Frenchy deliberately shot him in the back at the corner of Lowe and Main Streets. The Frenchman was jailed and then lynched by the "601 Vigilantes Committee" before he could even go to trial. An investigation into Frenchy's death was made and the records of the Justice of the Peace stated: "Case dis-missed as the defendant was taken out and hanged by a mob."

Bodie's residents consumed whiskey day and night; it was found to be as good for warding off pneumonia as for snakebite and was shipped into camp hundreds of barrels at a time. In Chinatown, dope was as popular as whiskey as a general cure-all, and opium dens (or bunks) were almost as commonplace as bars, or saloons. One opium user was Shotgun Johnny, also the town's undertaker, who dealt in used caskets. Johnny acquired his coffins secondhand by robbing graves, reburying the bodies, sanding the used coffins, and reselling them later. Johnny was described by one who knew him as an "undertaker by trade, a rounder by profession, a thief by inclination, a dope fiend by choice, and a scalawag by associations." Eventually, he was found on a Chinese bunk, dead from an overdose of opium or morphine or a combination of both.

More than $100 million worth of gold and silver was extracted from Bodie's mines. To keep the miners satisfied, Bodie had 65 saloons, 7 breweries, a soda pop plant, numerous hotels, and strings of wagon trains supplying them with the fuel—both of the alcoholic and the wood-burning variety—they needed in winter.

Winter was the real scourge of Bodie where snows driven by 100-mile-an-hour winds and minus 40-degree Fahrenheit temperatures left snowbanks sometimes 20 feet deep. Preparing for a Bodie winter was a monumental task. A railroad was built into Bodie—not to take ore out, but for the sole purpose of bringing in firewood. "I only know one place where the climate is likely to be more disagreeable, and that is the sulphury regions where we are informed on good authority that there is weeping and wailing and gnashing of teeth" (*Bodie Weekly Gazette*, 1879). At one winter christening, and the natives swore to this, it was so cold that the holy water froze and left an icicle hanging from the infant's chin.

Life was not easy for the citizens of Bodie.

1878: "Really, we can't say. It must be the altitude. There is some irresistible power in Bodie that impells us to cut and shoot each other to pieces."

1879: "There has been a rise in wood stealing. A man living in the south of town took a stick of wood lying handy on a neighbor's pile. It burnt very well until the giant powder cartridge in the end of the wood went off. The stove and a section of the roof went with it."

1881: "Stage robberies every two or three days seems to be the occupation of the unemployed."

1884: "In addition to two sirens of easy conscience being pitched out of a saloon head first through a glass door, a terrific war of words, with which all the expletives known to seven languages, was exchanged on Virtue Street."

Daybreak at Bodie

More than $100,000,000 in gold and silver were taken from Bodie mines.

In 1878 the town of Bodie boasted of having the "wickedest men, the wildest streets, and the worst climate out-of-doors."

Devils Postpile

In the midst of the forest and lake country west of Mammoth Lakes and a few miles southeast of Yosemite, there is a remarkable geological oddity known as Devils Postpile. What makes this structure so unique is its symmetrical basaltic columns that rise more than 60 feet into the air. These columns are linked together in honeycomb fashion, making them resemble a giant pipe organ. This massive cliff of lava columns is one of the three best examples of this type of structure known to exist in the world.

According to one early newspaper account, Devils Postpile was formed when "liquid lava flowed in a molten torrent from a nearby crater, plunged over a precipice, split into prisms, and hardened in mid-air." This account proved to be inaccurate, however, and subsequent scientific studies gave rise to a more logical explanation of how this unusual geological formation came into being.

It is now believed that about a million years ago lava poured from vents in the Sierra Nevada to form a six-mile flow in the valley of the Middle Fork of the San Joaquin River. Then an even process of solidification began, starting from the surface of the flow and moving into the center. As the lava cooled, shrinkage produced a tension pattern, which like drying mud, was relieved by cracking. These cracks extended into the mass as the cooling progressed, forming the huge basaltic columns.

During the last ice age, 100,000 years ago, glaciers moved down over the lava. These huge rivers of ice, some as many as 1,000 feet thick, carved and ground away at the Postpile's deposits, exposing the columns to view.

The vertical wall of gray lava pillars is about 200 feet wide and 40 to 60 feet high. Huge broken fragments which have fallen away from the wall fill the slopes at the foot of the Postpile. The polygonal structures have three to seven sides with about 55 percent of them having six sides. Most of the columns are vertical, but some are curved and slanted as if they had been bent by shifting after cooling.

A short trail leads to the top of the Postpile where one can stand on the exposed upper sections of the columns. Having been worn level and polished by the grinding action of the glaciers, they give the appearance of a colossal mosaic-tile floor.

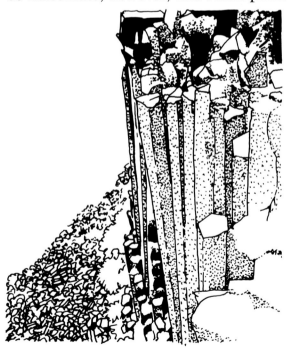

Devils Postpile

Viewed from the top, the columns resemble a mosaic-tile floor.

The Monument's gray lava pillars suggest a giant pipe organ.

Convict Lake, so named because it served as a hiding place for twenty-nine escaped convicts during the winter of 1871

Yosemite

"As I looked at the grandeur of the scene a peculiar exalted sensation seemed to fill my whole being, and I found my eyes in tears with emotion." Thus wrote one of the members of the first white party to explore Yosemite Valley in 1851.

Sculptured by ancient glaciers that are now sparkling streams, Yosemite National Park is undoubtedly one of nature's greatest achievements. Located in the heart of California's Sierra Nevada Mountains, millions travel from around the world to view its spectacular natural wonders.

Yosemite Valley is a glacier-cut gorge averaging 3,000 feet deep, about a mile wide, and 7 miles long. Its granite walls are sheer and bear the scars of the grinding glacial ice which pushed its way down the course of the Merced River some 30,000 years ago.

Among Yosemite's most distinguishing features are its granite formations and waterfalls, which rank high on the list of the world's greatest natural wonders. Yosemite Falls, the highest free-leaping waterfall in the world, drops 1,400 feet in one sheer fall, making it nine times higher than Niagara Falls. Other falls include the Merced River's Vernal and Nevada Falls and the graceful Bridalveil Falls.

Also within Yosemite Valley is the 7,500-foot El Capitan, which is the largest mountain of exposed granite in the world. At times sheer shafts of granite are formed, as in Sentinel Rock and Cathedral Spires. Other granite peaks form vast round domes; the most famous of these is Half Dome, which rises 3,000 feet above the floor of Yosemite Valley.

Glacier Point, above the Valley's rim, commands a magnificent view of the High Sierra and the valley below. It is a spectacle never to be forgotten, a panorama of domes, pinnacles, waterfalls, and peak upon peak of the crest of the Sierra.

The high country is another important part of Yosemite. Characterized by rugged peaks, glistening mountain lakes, and glacial polished granite, this unspoiled wilderness will delight those who wish to escape the crowded valley floor below. En route to Tuolumne Meadows, visitors can enjoy sweet-smelling forests, lush meadows, and the granite formations of the Lake Tenaya region.

A visit to Yosemite Valley is especially rewarding during the winter months when the crowds are gone and only the thunder of a distant avalanche or a wailing coyote disturbs the silence. Those who are lucky enough to be there when a winter storm is clearing, revealing a new-fallen snow and a deep blue sky with large billowing clouds, will have seen Yosemite at its grandest.

Half Dome

Yosemite Valley

Winter storm descends upon Sentinel Rock

Ominous clouds encircling Cathedral Spires

Bridalveil Falls

Snow-capped North Dome

Half Dome and Tenaya Canyon

Sunrise over Nevada and Vernal Falls as seen from Glacier Point

Trees grow out of cracks in granite formations at Tenaya Lake.

Gnarled Jeffrey pine growing atop Sentinel Dome

Mother Lode Country———————

When a settler named Jim Marshall picked up a shiny gold nugget from the stream at Sutter's Mill in 1848, he unleashed one of the greatest floods of humanity ever known. Fortune hunters from every corner of the world poured into California. Along the gulches and on the flats and river-bars of the Sierra Nevada, miners toiled with rockers and pans in a frenzied search for the gold-bearing Mother Lode veins.

The Mother Lode is actually a narrow strip of gold deposits about a mile wide and some 150 miles long that extends roughly from Mariposa to Auburn. But in popular vernacular, the term "Mother Lode Country" is used to refer to all the great mining regions of northern and central California.

From 1849 on, wide-open, rip-roaring mining towns sprang up everywhere throughout the Mother Lode Country, attracting miners from all over the country as well as the legendary characters for whom the California gold country is so well known. Among them were people like the sultry Lola Montez, the bandit Joaquin Murieta, the nefarious Black Bart, Three-fingered Jack, Madame Moustache, and Rattlesnake Dick. The

country abounds with legends about these characters, many of whom were immortalized by such writers as Mark Twain and Bret Harte.

Civilization came slowly to the mining camps, so miners devised their own codes and laws. Often, when there was serious trouble, the matter was settled by simply hanging the person who seemed the most deserving. But as San Francisco grew and prospered from the gold that came from the diggings, more civilized forms of law and order were brought to the mining camps.

Although entire towns grew up overnight, they often died just as quickly. In fact, more than half the original mining towns cannot even be found today. Because these ramshackle towns were largely constructed of canvas and wood planks, they were easy targets for rampaging fires. The miners themselves were often to blame for the fires, especially after a night of drinking and carousing in a saloon or dance hall.

After ten short years of feverish activity the cream was skimmed from the Mother Lode. The miners drifted away, leaving the landscape strewn with relics of their heroic labors—abandoned mine shafts, moldering sluiceways, and rusting mining equipment. In each of the remaining towns original buildings still stand, although new trees have grown and natural vegetation has covered the scarred earth that was once torn apart by the frenzied search for gold. Now, for the most part, the Mother Lode Country is as tranquil as it was before the whiskered gold seekers swarmed in with their picks and pans.

Wells Fargo building and stage depot in Columbia

Throughout the Motherlode Country old historical buildings and remnants of abandoned mining equipment are still visible.

Sequoia and Kings Canyon————

Immense rugged peaks, steep canyons, and awe-inspiring Big Trees set in a unique mountain wilderness make Sequoia and Kings Canyon National Parks among the most beautiful sights in California. In fact, the combined parks offer some of the most primitive natural scenery in the United States. Here, the streams of the Kings, Kern, and Kaweah Rivers have made their beds in the deep granite gorges that form the mighty canyons. But perhaps the most spectacular sight to behold in these parks is the 14,495-foot Mount Whitney, which is the highest peak in the United States outside Alaska.

Of all the living things which inhabit the slopes and crags of the Sierra Nevada, none has commanded as much attention as have the world-famous sequoias, or Big Trees (*Sequoia gigantia*), which are among the largest and oldest living organisms on earth. Although the Coast Redwood (*Sequoia semperviren*) is taller, rising 370 feet, the Big Tree is much more massive. The

mountain sequoia reaches a diameter of 35 feet and a height of 270 feet. Some are as many as 3,500 years old, second only to the bristlecone pine.

The sequoia has several unique characteristics that contribute to its longevity. Its thick, asbestos-like bark resists fire and various insect attacks. When fire, winds, or storms do cause damage, the sequoia demonstrates remarkable recuperative powers, growing new wood over fire scars and producing new branches and crowns to replace those broken by the elements.

The Big Trees can be found growing in isolated groves on ridges and plateaus throughout the Sierra, but they are most numerous in Sequoia National Park, where they form extensive forests. Naturalist John Muir, who was an ardent explorer of the area, named the largest of these groves the Giant Forest. The Big Trees in this forest are indeed giants among trees, with their deeply fluted, columnar trunks and cinnamon-colored bark. Even the trees' lowest branches loom high above the ground, their trunks disappearing into clouds of green foliage, making the treetops invisible. One experiences a profound sense of peace in the presence of these majestic trees.

Except for brief closings during and after the winter snows, both Sequoia and Kings Canyon National Parks are kept open throughout the year. In winter the sequoias are festooned with snow and the forest floor is covered with a trackless white blanket. The winter air is always crisp and a special stillness settles over the forests.

General Grant Tree, also known as the "Nation's Christmas Tree," is the second largest tree in the world.

Fallen Tree along Congress Trail

The House Group on the Congress Trail

A view of the Great Western Divide from Moro Rock

Morning sun illuminates forest foliage.

Winter in General Grant Grove

Mineral King

Remote Mineral King Valley is made up of peaks, cirques, cliffs, and high passes from which streams cascade and tumble. It is a spot that has known the mark of civilization for nearly a hundred years and yet it remains unspoiled. Its wild rugged beauty is much the same today as it must have been when white men first discovered the valley in the 1860s.

Mountains loom everywhere as one first enters the Mineral King Valley. To the south are Bandever and Florence Peaks with Farewell Gap inviting hikers to come and explore beyond. To the north lies Timber Gap. In the east, Sawtooth Peak, a landmark in the high country, stands next to Mineral Peak and Empire Mountain. To the west is a high ridge and the route to Eagle, Mosquito, White Chief, and many other alpine lakes. The

stream that meanders down the middle of the Valley makes up the East Fork of the Kaweah River.

Riding and hiking trails reach up out of the Valley in every direction leading to the high country of the Sierra Nevada. A view of the rugged granite land beyond the Valley awaits those who are adventurous enough to spend many hours afoot or on horseback.

In the year 1880, a wagon road was built into Mineral King for mining and logging purposes. Although the road was reconstructed in 1923, it remains much the same today as it was then. Hundreds of curves lie ahead when one turns off the highway for Mineral King. The slim, 25-mile-long passageway is so narrow that it is difficult to negotiate by automobile, and takes over two hours to drive safely. However, the view improves with each mile as the road winds up into the canyon of the East Fork of the Kaweah River. Groves of Big Trees, rusting mining equipment, forested ridges, and silhouetted ridgetops are only a few of the outstanding sights found along this winding canyon road.

The moisture caught by the Sierra Nevada keeps the Valley luxuriously green throughout the summer. Deep winter snows make the road inaccessible during eight months of the year. This long respite from human contact keeps the Valley unspoiled and helps preserve the delicate balance required for living things to maintain their complex relationships.

Mineral King is one of the few remaining true mountain sanctuaries.

Bandever and Florence Peaks serve as a backdrop for the southern end of Mineral King Valley.

A stately bridge along the old wagon road that crosses the East Fork of the Kaweah River.

Monarch Creek Falls

Summer cloudburst clearing over Monarch Minaret

Summer cabins dot the landscape at the northern end of the Valley.

High country near Eagle Lake

Owens Valley

Just beyond the steep crest of the Sierra Nevada, the world seems to drop off abruptly. From an alpine domain of snow-covered peaks the precipitous eastern wall of the Sierra Nevada plunges two miles down into the desert. Nowhere else in the state is there such a sudden contrast of geography. The deep trench of Owens Valley runs parallel to the Sierra's east wall for 125 miles. Just east of the Sierra Nevada's bold alpine crest rises another mighty range that is almost as high—the White-Inyo Mountains. The highest peaks of both ranges, Mount Whitney and White Mountain Peak, stand well over 14,000 feet. The Owens Valley, which is only twenty miles wide, serves to separate these two lofty ranges.

On the flat level plain of Owens Valley the Alabama Hills, northwest of Lone Pine, rise above the valley floor, but they are dwarfed by the great bordering mountain ranges. The hills are weather-worn decomposed granite rock formations believed by some to be among the oldest rock formations on the North American continent. From the Alabama Hills the road extends on to Whitney Portal. The Portal, which is usually the eastern point of departure for hikers

backpacking into the Sierras, offers an excellent view of Mount Whitney and the six peaks that surround the summit.

Because the height and shape of the Sierra Nevada wring most of the moisture out of the clouds, the Valley is left parched. By 9:00 A.M. on midsummer mornings the temperature in the Valley is usually over 100 degrees Fahrenheit. Visitors are advised to plan their trips in accordance with seasonal temperatures to avoid discomfort and to best enjoy the delights of this unique region.

On those cold winter mornings when fresh snow has fallen on the Sierra crest one sees the Valley at its best. The ranges on either side are fantasylands of dazzling white peaks. You may be fortunate enough to be there immediately following a winter storm, when the snowline is only slightly above the Valley's floor, or on a rare day when the snow banners fly from the highest peaks of the crest.

Owens Valley was once the scene of bitter warfare between the farmers who had settled there and the city of Los Angeles, which was seeking to confine the waters that drain off the Sierra to supply the city's population. Ranching, which began in the late 1800s, flourished in Owens Valley until the city of Los Angeles finally acquired its water rights and built an aqueduct to transport the water to the growing urban area. In protest, night riders placed high-powered explosives along the aqueduct system, charging that their land and water rights had been "stolen" by the city. And to this day there are still hard feelings between the two factions.

Mount Whitney, at an elevation of 14,495 feet, and the tall peaks that surround it

Winter storm comes to a climax
along the eastern edge of the Sierra

The Alabama Hills, actually weathered granite rock
formations, lie at the base of the snow-clad Sierra Nevada.

Bristlecone Pines

There is an ancient forest where the land and sky are continually purified by the relentless icy winds, rain, sleet, and snow, where exotic seeds fall and are swept by the winds until they settle in unfriendly soil. Here they mingle with rain and the moisture from melting snow until they germinate and burst forth through glacier gravel into the rarefied air of 12,000 feet. It is a place where one can find trees that were living 2,500 years before Christ. It is the ancient Bristlecone Pine Forest of the White Mountains, 20 miles east of the Sierra Nevada.

Bristlecone pines were here when the pyramids of Egypt were being built by the Hebrew slaves. They had already been in existence for many years when Moses received the Ten Commandments on Mount Sinai. They were several hundred years old when the lordly legions of Rome battled with Gaul. When the three wise men followed their star to Bethlehem, the bristlecone pines were growing in a

remote mountain land unknown in those times, a land that would one day be called California.

Temperatures in this area are severe and the terrain is sculptured and polished by the elements, blasted by sand and sleet, and warped by wind and water. The pines themselves have been distorted into "living ruins." Many of the trees, though beautifully shaped and unusual in form, appear to be dead until one looks more closely and discovers a small strand of bark twisting around a trunk to the one side or a branch that is still surviving. Many of the trees are more dead than alive. How do they live to be 4,500 years old?

The amazing longevity of these pines is usually attributed to the fact that they have always had to cope with unusually harsh conditions. In an environment of poor rocky soil, a short growing season, scanty precipitation, and violent winter gales, the bristlecone pines have been forced to battle for life throughout the ages. While other types of trees, many of them more favorably situated, have proliferated for several generations and then died out, this hardy species developed the ability to suspend its growth during extremely dry periods, adding only an inch or less of new rings each hundred years. It is significant that the oldest specimens occupy the driest, most unfavorable sites where the growth rate is the slowest. So fierce is their determination to survive that some wind-blown specimens have grown parallel to the earth rather than give in to the forces of nature. It is also noteworthy that the cones of many of the oldest trees still produce fertile seeds. These stunted pines of the upper timber zone grow to heights of only 20 to 40 feet while across the Sierra the giant sequoia reaches heights of 200 to 275 feet.

Tree ring dating of the bristlecone pines, which is accomplished by taking a small core sample from the tree, is of tremendous scientific value in that it provides an extremely accurate record of past climatic conditions in the dry Southwest. Such records have numerous applications to agriculture, wildlife management, and the management of our public lands. Tree ring analysis might also enable scientists to predict long-term water yields in the Southwest. Some of the dead trees date back more than 6,600 years, and one of these may be the link that will extend the records of climate back to the end of the last ice age 10,000 years ago.

The oldest trees are found in Schulman Grove. One of the most famous of these is Pine Alpha, a 4,300-year-old tree named after the first letter in the Greek Alphabet. A rugged two-mile trail leads to Methuselah Walk from Schulman Grove. The Methuselah tree, which is the oldest living organism known to exist in the world, is 4,600 years old.

A twisted pine along Methuselah Walk in Schulman Grove.

Bristlecone pines grow in the rarefied air of 12,000-foot elevations.

*Assaulted by the elements, the pines' trunks assume
odd shapes and take on fascinating colors.*

Because of their remarkable longevity – some are known to be over 4,500 years old–these trees have been referred to as "living ruins."

The Desert and Southern Coastland

The desert has long had a certain mystery associated with it. Simultaneously fascinating and repelling, this hot, dry wasteland with its barren mud hills, slot-like canyons, spiny plants, and endless shifting sands creates an atmosphere of desolation that keeps the uninitiated away. Yet for those who are rugged and adventurous enough to explore and get to know it, the desert is a land of striking beauty characterized by contrasts of incredible color and land formations.

The California Desert is a unique storehouse of historical, geological, and geographical treasures, offering innumerable opportunities for mining, scientific exploration, and nature study. But its greatest value lies in the fact that it is a wilderness where unusual, highly adapted plants and animals coexist in a complex and fascinating ecological relationship that is still not completely understood by scientists.

Contrary to popular belief, the desert is not flat, but is composed of range after range of sculptured mountains, whose features have been carved by centuries of wind and water. Here one can observe nature actively at work. Although the desert is a land of little rain, water plays a continuous role in shaping, arranging, and rearranging the landscape. Occasional winter showers and sudden cloudbursts carve deep canyons and washes in the sedimentary deposits, forming badlands and mudhills; in other areas the sandstones are scoured by the water into beautiful hills. Wind is also a powerful erosional force, particularly in areas where the vegetation is too sparse to provide adequate protection. Because the surface soil and sand are usually dry, frequent winds can easily pick them up from one place and redeposit them in another; sand dunes are a characteristic result of the work of wind. Wind-born particles of sand also act as abrasive agents which blast against desert formations, constantly shaping and reforming them.

From Death Valley the California Desert stretches south 240 miles to the border of Mexico. From the Colorado River, it rolls west to the slopes of the Sierra Madre, San Gabriel, San Bernardino, San Jacinto, and Laguna Mountains that protect the southern California coastlands from the desert's heat. Inside these

boundaries the California Desert is subdivided into two geographic areas—the Mojave and the Colorado Deserts, as indicated on the map.

The Mojave Desert (or high desert) is an upland desert with elevations ranging from 1,000 to 6,000 feet above sea level. The one exception is Badwater in Death Valley, which at 282 feet below sea level is the lowest spot in the western hemisphere.

In contrast, the Colorado Desert (or low desert) lies either below sea level or just slightly above it. Due to extreme desert conditions, vegetation here is sparse. This region is especially noted for Anza-Borrego State Park.

Around the eastern edge of southern California looms a vast amphitheater of mountains, composed of a series of ranges. These mountains mark the end of the desert and begin a 50-mile descent to the Pacific Ocean. Between the mountains and the ocean, one finds miles of unspoiled backcountry, with rambling hills, meadows, and a series of ranches and farming valleys. In the vicinity around Los Angeles the mountain terrain is steep and ends in broad, flat plains that are famous for their fruit orchards.

Death Valley

Ever since the first white men arrived in Death Valley, fantastic tales have been told of its blasting temperatures and hidden treasures. But exaggeration is inevitable in describing this unique, 150-mile-long, narrow valley of varicolored geography which lies shimmering between steep and rocky mountain ranges.

Death Valley was once part of an inland sea until violent earth movements, which occurred some millions of years ago, spawned majestic mountain ranges known today as the Panamint, Amargosa, and Last Chance. The sea was ultimately dried up by the blistering desert sun, leaving behind an abundance of rich mineral deposits, such as borax, copper, silver, gold, and fantastic salt flats.

During the winter months the Valley's temperatures hover in the mid-80s. During the summer, however, the Valley is transformed into a raging inferno, the heat at times reaching temperatures as high as 134 degrees Fahrenheit.

Because it ranges in width from only six to fifteen miles, the barren mountains

are always visible on the horizon. In winter they rise up from the Valley in snow-tipped elegance; in summer they glimmer from the waves of heat that rise from the salt flats below. The mountain walls and valleys are a visual display of multi-colored hues. The green and blue of copper, yellow of sulphur, red of hematite and cinnabar, and white of salt and borax blend with the black and gray of the desolate rocks and the royal purple and pale green of the mineral-stained granites.

Although famed as a scene of cruel heat, which brought suffering and death to the early immigrants and gold miners, Death Valley's sinister reputation is not entirely deserved. Early written accounts tell of death and tortures from thirst and heat "too horrible to print" and of deadly vapors and poisonous dust carried by the winds, "which, if inhaled, will eat the vitals and eventually rob one of life." But, in truth, Death Valley's record of human lives lost, measured against that of the rest of the western desert, is unimpressive. Still, the region remains associated with death. Such names as Dead Man's Gulch, Coffin Canyon, Funeral Mountains, Suicide Spring, Devil's Golf Course, Hell Gate, and the Last Chance Range all help to preserve Death Valley's image.

It was borax that was finally responsible for the partial taming of the Valley. In the 1880s, "cottonball" borax was refined at the Harmony Borax Works and freighted over 165 miles of agonizing desert in huge high-wheeled wagons drawn by 20-mule teams.

Sand dunes near Stovepipe Wells

Spiny salt formation at Devil's Golf Course

Badwater, at 282 feet below sea level, is the lowest point in the continental United States.

*Zabriskie Point and the yellow
mudhills of Golden Canyon*

Striped Butte rises 4,500 feet above the floor of Butte Valley.

Monument's growing burro population is causing concern among ecologists, who fear the animals are upsetting the area's ecological balance.

Mitchell Caverns

Mitchell Caverns is located in the center of a vast, arid, sparsely populated portion of the eastern Mojave Desert. Because it is virtually isolated from other communities, without even a major highway close by, the few local residents call the area "lonesome triangle." This sun-scorched land is made up of broad valleys filled with creosote bush and cactus, sand dunes, cinder cones, and dramatic desert mountain ranges. The 5,200-acre State Reserve is situated on the eastern slope of the Providence Mountains where the land sweeps up from Clipper Valley to high, heavily weathered rhyolite crags reaching 7,171 feet in elevation.

The caverns for which the park is named are filled with intricate limestone formations and remain at a nearly constant temperature of 65 degrees Fahrenheit throughout the year. El Pakiva and Tecopa Caverns are open to the public and have been equipped with stairs and special lighting.

The name El Pakiva comes from the Chemehuevi Indian word meaning "Devil's House." Over the ages, water dripping from the cave's limestone ceiling has formed a grotto which has a main chamber that is 200 feet long and filled with varied limestone formations shaped like cauliflower heads, mushrooms, bowls of spaghetti, and flat shields resembling artists' palettes. Throughout the caverns icicle-shaped stalactites hang down from the ceilings and stalagmites extend upward from the floor.

Deep inside the cavern one walks through a tunnel to the second cave, which is known as Tecopa. Tecopa's ceiling in its main chamber is twenty-nine feet high. Artifacts found in the cave, which was once inhabited by Native Americans, are now on display in the park's visitor center.

Archeological work in the caverns turned up the bones of a Pleistocene ground sloth, one of the prehistoric animals that apparently roamed this territory and occasionally made use of the caverns some ten to fifteen thousand years ago. The Native American artifacts suggest that humans have been using the caverns for at least 500 years. The smoke-blackened walls, hidden caches of food, tools, and other evidence of habitation show that the Chemehuevi used the caverns, at least on a seasonal basis, while hunting for game and as storage places for their collections of nuts from the piñon pine and the many other desert plants which they used for food or medicine.

*The main chamber of El Pakiva Cavern is noted
for its varied and unusual limestone formations.*

Pointed and spear-like stalactites protect passageways leading into Tecopa Cavern.

Icicle-shaped stalagmites and stalactites characterize this section of Tecopa Canyon.

Fluted, brightly colored sandstone layers at Redrock Canyon

Abandoned hard-rock mine shaft in erosion-carved canyon near Butterbread Peak

Joshua Tree

When the first white explorers arrived in California's vast Mojave desert country in 1855, they discovered thousands of giant yucca plants, some of which rose to heights of up to 40 feet. Because these unusual plants seemed to have their arms spread to the heavens as though in prayer, they soon became known as the "praying plants." Some years later, they were given the name Joshua tree by a Mormon visitor who felt that the giant cactus seemed to be lifting its branches to heaven, pointing the way to the promised land. To many desert dwellers the Joshua tree, actually a member of the lily family, is indeed something of a "heavenly" plant. Not only does it provide shelter and food but in some cases even protection from enemies. Local Native Americans were perhaps the first to realize the

vast resources of the plant. In addition to using parts of it for food, they made ropes and woven articles from its leaves, obtained various dyes and medicines from its roots, and even brewed an intoxicating beverage from its fruit.

In spring the Joshua tree bears creamy white blossoms in clusters eight to fourteen inches long. The number of grotesque shapes it can assume is infinite, and its other unusual properties have long made it a popular subject of study among scientists and other curiosity seekers.

Hundreds of other species of desert plants join the Joshuas in Joshua Tree National Monument, a strikingly beautiful and serene setting that covers half a million acres and ranges in altitude from 1,000 to 6,000 feet. Its strange rock formations, some over 500 million years old, its abandoned mines, and its spectacular view points continue to lure visitors to the region. Also of interest are the simple, "homemade" gravestones that supposedly mark the spot where hopeful gold miners gave up their futile quest for riches, died, and were buried.

Another noteworthy sight in the monument is Hidden Valley, a beautiful oasis concealed from view by a shield of rock formations. Oldtimers tell stories of how cattle rustlers used to lead their herds into the valley through a narrow passageway, hiding them there until it was safe to dispose of them. The quiet in the valley is almost eerie and not much imagination is needed to conjure up images of the dangers associated with cattle thievery many years ago.

These giant yuccas, called "praying plants" by early settlers, are known to reach heights of 40 feet.

Rock formations that are millions of years old are found throughout the park.

In spring the Joshua trees bear creamy white blossoms 8 to 14 inches long.

Anza Borrego

Anza-Borrego Desert State Park derives its name from the Spanish explorer Juan Bautista de Anza and from the Spanish word, *borrego*, which means bighorn sheep, a dying breed of animals that still inhabit the park's mountain wilderness. In 1775, Colonel Anza led a party of Spanish settlers from Santa Fe to the settlement of San Francisco, opening the first trail through the treacherous desert that is now known as Anza-Borrego. Some years later the Mormon Batallion, following basically the same route, carved a trail for their wagons from the rocky side of a shallow canyon. That trail can still be seen today on the side of Box Canyon. Eventually, the famous Butterfield stages crossed through the area, as did thousands of others en route to the promised land of California.

Parts of the Anza-Borrego Desert offer an astounding array of diverse plant life. In springtime, its seemingly barren areas literally spring to life with a variety of shrubs, plants, and flowers. After a wet winter, the desert floor is carpeted with magnificent wildflowers and other forms of vegetation. When temperature

and rainfall conditions are right, seeds that have lain dormant for years seem to spring into being.

In shallow ravines and isolated mountain canyons, where the water comes to the surface, fan palms can be found either growing by themselves or in colonies. These palms attain heights of 80 to 100 feet and may live more than 200 years. Desert Native American tribes made good use of the leaves to thatch their huts and made rope and twine from the fibers.

The half-million-acre park contains a wide variety of scenic features that offer a striking combination of mountain and desert landscapes. Unusual geological formations add striking contrasts to the desert. Curious sandstone formations, mud caverns, and the remains of ancient lakes set a dramatic stage for clear skies and colorful sunrises and sunsets.

Most landforms in the desert have been produced by a combination of weathering, mass movements, landslides, mud flows, and running water. Ravines, ridges, and arroyos are typical of desert landscapes formed by sudden desert cloudbursts and the subsequent rapid runoff. The badlands at Font's Point are partly the result of this sort of conditioning.

Wind is also an effective agent of erosion. Small sand particles carried by the wind act as abrasives which sandblast desert forms into odd shapes. The Pumpkin Patch is an example of a soft outer material being sandblasted and eroded away from a harder core material to assume the shape of giant pumpkins in a field.

Pumpkin Patch, created over the years by wind and water erosion.

Isolated Palm Canyon, with its steep ravines, houses over 1,000 fan palms.

The trees in Palm Canyon may reach heights of 80 to 100 feet and live to be over 200 years old.

Western descent into Borrego Valley

View of Borrego Badlands from Font's Point.

Southern Coastland

Around the eastern edge of southern California are a series of mountain ranges that mark the end of the desert. In these mountains nature enthusiasts can hike over hundreds of miles of trails, fish in numerous lakes and streams, or enjoy snow sports in the winter. For the casual visitor, there are short, scenic walks through fragrant woodlands and scenic drives to easily accessible lakes, towns, and historical areas. The mountain foothills offer rural country lanes that travel through rambling hills, meadows, and farm lands.

From Santa Barbara to San Diego the ocean and coastline present a variety of sights. Mile after mile of smooth, sandy beaches characterize the southern California coastline. But not all the coast is open beach. Sporadic sea bluffs, some more than 300 feet high, tower above the surf and add variety to the seashore. One of the more famous bluff areas is found at Torrey Pines State Reserve. Here eroded sandstone sea bluffs drop into the Pacific in a glorious array of color and form.

The California coastline provides some of the most fascinating natural communities in the state, reflecting the great wealth of living organisms present in the ocean. The most accessible of these are found along the southern coast, where even the smallest tidepools are worth investigating for their rich assortment of sea life. In no other place can one see more animals in a single visit. Tidepools are readily visible, and their inhabitants are for the most part large enough to be easily observed. The best time for exploration is during low tide when one can venture out to rocks and reefs to discover tiny colonies of sea life.

One does not have to travel a great distance in southern California to find natural beauty. The country backroads, the seashore, and the mountains are all located within a concentrated area, and the southern cities have outstanding parks and natural areas, for those interested enough to explore them.

Monarch butterflies along their annual migratory route between central California and Mexico.

Unusual cliff formations and sea caves along the La Jolla coastline

Coastal tidepools

Santa Barbara backcountry

Ranunculus grow in belt-like patterns near the Carlsbad coast.

Torrey Pines

Torrey Pines State Reserve is a majestic wilderness park that stretches along the coast just north of San Diego. Its fragile environment provides a home for the world's rarest pine tree, the *Pinus torreyana*. At one time, perhaps as many as 10,000 years ago, these trees may have covered a large part of southern California, but today they grow naturally only here, at Torrey Pines State Reserve, and on Santa Rosa Island, which lies some 175 miles to the northwest in the Pacific.

Neither soil, climate, nor civilization has lent a helping hand to the surviving trees, now confined to only a thousand acres. The stand that once stretched some twenty miles along the coast was rapidly depleted by Native Americans, Spaniards, and other early inhabitants of the area, who regularly used the pines for firewood. Later, when the rarity of these trees was recognized, steps were taken to protect them and the canyoned mesa on which they stand.

Today the Reserve is much as it was a hundred years ago, when it was described by one observer as "a series of high, broken cliffs and deeply indented ravines on the bold headlands overlook-

ing the sea, with the trees clinging to the face of the crumbling sandstone."

The trees themselves take on a variety of unusual shapes—bent, twisted, or gnarled—as dictated by the elements. Where most exposed to wind and salty air, especially along the great sea bluff that rises 300 feet above the surf, they may reach heights of only 10 feet. In contrast, a torrey pine planted in Carpinteria, California, in 1890 is now close to 100 feet tall.

Of particular interest is the Guy Fleming Trail, which winds through the North Grove area of the Reserve. Unusual forms of torrey pines can be seen on the half-mile loop trail that parallels the bluffs overlooking the sea and offers a panorama of the Pacific and coastal landmarks.

Other trails in the park tend to follow natural, weatherworn paths. One such trail, appropriately called "Fat Man's Misery," winds along a deep canyon carved out of the sandstone by rainwater trickling toward the coast over the course of many centuries. The name is fitting since the width of this narrow canyon is in some places barely more than a foot, with sandstone cliffs rising straight up 30 to 40 feet on both sides.

Also within Torrey Pines Park is Penasquitos Marsh Natural Preserve, which forms one of the last remaining waterfowl refuges in southern California. The marsh and lagoon provide a home for several rare and endangered species of birds and serve as a vital stopping or nesting place for many migratory waterfowl.

A lone torrey pine standing on a high bluff at the Pacific's edge

School children enjoy the coastline scenery after exploring the Reserve

Solemn moonlit pine

Pacific sunsets at Torrey Pines Reserve

A hang glider rides on the air currents rising from Torrey Pines bluffs.

Torrey pines grow naturally only here and on Santa Rosa island 175 miles to sea.

The Big Sur Coastline

It has been said that "Big Sur is a state of mind, not a place." Almost everyone who visits Big Sur succumbs to the spell of its violent yet soothing mixture of mountain and sea. It is a craggy coast characterized by supremely beautiful and wild ruggedness, a region where mountains sheer off into the Pacific, where rock, promontory, headland, and twisted tree know the battle-sting of strong winds and an aggressive sea.

Ridges of the Santa Lucia Range buttress the rough cliffs of Big Sur as if to protect the headland from the violent force of the Pacific. It is a land of savage winter storms and striking scenery. The wild, steep Santa Lucia Mountains and raw Pacific meet in a collision of color and sound that is disturbing and yet alluring.

The moods of Big Sur change with the weather, according to season, month, day, and hour. In winter, the assault on the terrain is horrendous. Storms blast in and tear at the rocks and shallow canyons, sometimes ripping out parts of the road and destroying bridges. These great Pacific storms are as violent as the scenery. In summer the fog rolls quietly up the mountain walls, smothering everything in sight, while the sea roars unseen. The rocks drip, seals bark, gulls and loons cry, and foghorns on lonesome crags moan their warning to ships offshore.

"One common note of all this country," observed Robert Louis Stevenson, "is the haunting presence of the ocean. Everywhere, even in quiet weather, the low, distant, thrilling roar of the Pacific hangs over the coast and the adjacent country like smoke above the battle."

Over the years, Big Sur has remained as wild and undeveloped as when Gespar De Portola first pushed his weary way through its virgin territory in 1769. In exploring and settling California, the Spanish remained in the Big Sur area only long enough to give it its name, which means "Big South." Much later, the homesteaders traveled here by land, and for a while sailing schooners brought in cotton goods and food in exchange for lumber and mineral deposits. The area remained ruggedly primitive and remote until 1937 when a two-lane highway was constructed. Prior to that time, the only land access had been over tortuous mountain trails by horseback and mule. "They train a mule," so the legend went, "to bring in the school teacher. Then they shoot the mule and marry the school teacher."

Big Sur retains most of the plant and wildlife that was here in the days of the early settlers. The mountainsides are covered with wildflowers, lilac bushes, and redwood trees; coyotes, wildcats, mountain lions, wild boars, and rattlesnakes maintain an existence in the hills; and migratory animals traveling north or south still convene in this isolated area. Not far off the shore one can hear the sounds of seals, sea otters, and sea lions, and at certain times of the year the great gray whale swims close to shore headed for its Mexican breeding ground. Overhead and beside the sea, land birds—the hawk, the buzzard, and the golden eagle—soar.

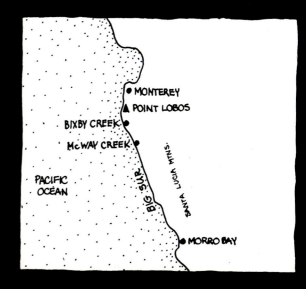

Big Sur, lying at the narrow edge of this huge continent, seems to resist progress, achieving unparalled natural beauty. In deep, dark gorges covered with fern fronds and dotted with wild calla lillies, in the song of tiny mountain streams trickling down to the sea, in the deep forest shade sliced with cathedral sunlight is what Robinson Jeffers called the "sacred calm." Here, one experiences a profound peace, an almost religious feeling, and the simple wisdom of unspoiled wilderness.

The ever-present, sparkling Pacific Ocean

The wild Santa Lucia Mountains buttress the coastline.

A tiny path leading through the carpeted forest floor

Redwood stands grow in selected canyons at the edge of their southern boundary.

Bixby Creek and the Pacific shoreline

It is not uncommon for the weather to change at a moment's notice.

Farms such as this one recall the days when early settlers inhabited Big Sur.

McWay Creek rushes down the slopes of the Santa Lucia Mountains.

At the end of its journey McWay Creek glides over a granite ledge to become one of the few waterfalls to drop into the Pacific Ocean.

From each ridge and ravine–and there are thousands of them–come tiny streams such as this one.

The rare combination of headlands, mountains, and sea provides striking scenery.

The sea's constant motion carves out beaches and grottos.

*The forests and mountainsides are much the same
as they were when early explorers first arrived.*

Point Lobos

A rocky promontory at the northern end of Big Sur, Point Lobos State Reserve has long been recognized as a setting of rare natural beauty. The noted landscape artist, Francis McComas, described it as "the greatest meeting of land and water in the world," extravagant praise to be accorded any one portion of the earth's surface, yet all those who come here agree that the beauty of this headland is unequaled.

Point Lobos derives its name from its numerous colonies of California and Steller's sea lions, whose hoarse barking sounds carry inland from the offshore

rocks at Punta de los Lobos Marinos, which in Spanish means Point of the Seawolves.

Scientists are particularly interested in Point Lobos because of the sea lions and sea otters that live here. Point Lobos is also the northernmost breeding place of the California brown pelican as well as the home of many other forms of land and marine life that coexist in remarkable relationship to their environment and to each other.

Perhaps the most outstanding feature of the Reserve is its groves of Monterey cypress. In earlier geological times the Monterey cypress was widely distributed throughout California, but now it is making a last stand in the Monterey region. Clinging to the cliffs above the surf, distorted by wind and weather, and often shrouded in drifting fog, the trees tell of the never-ending conflict between sea and land. The still-living trees are rich with green foliage; the dead are stark in silhouette, their bleached and twisted branches red with algae.

It seems miraculous that Point Lobos escaped destruction during the years it was passed almost haphazardly from one owner to another. Once, in the free and easy days of the Mexican regime, it changed hands in a game of cards. Over the years, Point Lobos has been the site of a whaling station, an abalone cannery, and a shipping point for a coal mine; it has been proposed as a townsite, grazed over by cattle, and occasionally burned. Finally, in 1933, it was acquired by the state of California, its essential, primitive character still intact.

Monterey cypress cling to cliffs above the surf.

The "Old Veteran" stands alone at the head of Little Dome's cove.

Sculptured rock formations slope into the Pacific.

Portuguese whalers' cottage at Whaler's Cove

Monterey Cypress making a last stand along the Monterey coast

The North Coast and Redwoods

Northward up the coast of California, a progressive change takes place, a change that is especially noticeable in the appearance of the land and in the feel of the wind and sun. The climate becomes cooler and damper. The ocean currents grow cold and forbidding while intermittent fog rolls in off the threatening surf, dampening the coastal belt and nourishing the land. It is here that redwood forests plunge down canyons into the sea, uninhabited headlands reach out into the exploding breakers, and weather-beaten towns display an air of timeless dignity. The area's rich history is emphasized when one recalls that the flags of England, Spain, Mexico, Russia, and the California Republic have flown here.

The jagged shoreline is characteristic of the rugged North Coast. Cliffs and mountains rise streaming from the sea, sculpturing the coastline with rocky, studded covers. Occasionally, the headlands open for narrow river inlets where prosperous fishing villages cling protectively to the shelter of the shore. For countless centuries, this coastal area has taken the full strength of the powerful Pacific swells as they rise out of the turbulent sea and release their fury upon the land.

The works of civilization add a nostalgic note to the landscape, as evidenced by the settlements of now-weathered storefronts, steepled churches, and gabled houses built by an earlier generation. Old farm buildings rest behind stately rows of dark, tangled cypress trees. Abandoned wharves, lumber mills, and New England-looking towns recall the days when great quantities of lumber were processed and shipped from the once busy villages along this shore.

The great coast redwood groves (*Sequoia sempervirens*) are perhaps the most awe-inspiring of the many dramatic sights in the North Coast region. The redwoods are a unique forest spectacle with their giant fluted trunks, some rising more than 360 feet in height and reaching 40 feet in diameter. With high majestic crowns swaying in the wind, they catch and filter the earthbound sunlight like stained glass windows in a great cathedral. Nearly as old as Western Civilization, with many specimens dating back to before the birth of Christ, these trees humble the reverent viewer with their antiquity and majestic proportions.

The Roads

For two hundred crooked miles, from San Francisco to Westport, California's historic Highway 1 clings precipitously to the North Coast edge. It is narrow, winding, and potentially dangerous as it climbs mountain ledges that drop directly into the sea. It has numerous blind curves, a noticeable absence of guard rails, and herds of loose farm animals grazing along its path. But Highway 1 possesses the grace of a delicate river as it hugs the natural contours of the coast, flowing across ravines on arched bridges and passing great stands of eucalyptus and cypress and scatterings of redwood growth. It meanders by cattle and sheep ranges and farmlands that roll upwards from the logged coastal shelf to forest-fringed hills. It skirts large, shallow bays where offshore oyster beds are fenced in by long rows of slender stakes. There are still small towns, lonely farms, and fences that have withstood a century of blowing winds generated by the fury of the Pacific Ocean along this route. After reaching Westport, Highway 1 turns inland and meets the famous Redwood Highway (U.S. 101) as it travels through the heart of California's best coastal redwood forests on its way to the Oregon border.

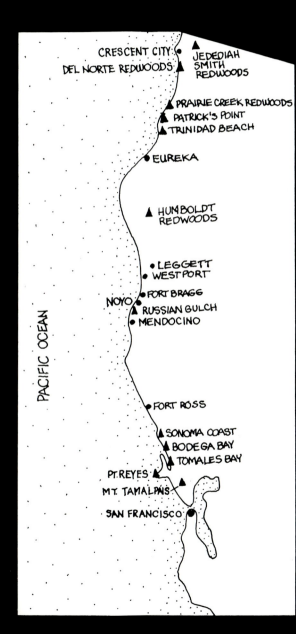

CRESCENT CITY
DEL NORTE REDWOODS
JEDEDIAH SMITH REDWOODS
PRAIRIE CREEK REDWOODS
PATRICK'S POINT
TRINIDAD BEACH
EUREKA
HUMBOLDT REDWOODS
LEGGETT
WESTPORT
FORT BRAGG
NOYO
RUSSIAN GULCH
MENDOCINO
FORT ROSS
SONOMA COAST
BODEGA BAY
TOMALES BAY
PT. REYES
MT. TAMALPAIS
SAN FRANCISCO
PACIFIC OCEAN

Mount Tamalpais

Jutting 2,604 feet above sea level, Mount Tamalpais commands a sweeping panorama of the surrounding hills, forests, and sea. It stands as a lofty landmark for local residents and travelers, who frequently scale its slopes to gain an unbroken view of land and water that seems nearly endless. On a clear day, Mount Shasta can be seen 200 miles to

the north, the Sierra Nevada Range 60 miles to the east, and the Santa Cruz Mountains 50 miles to the south. From the summit, the Pacific and the whole sweep of the San Francisco Bay, including several islands and 100 miles of rolling hills lie at the viewer's feet.

Because the Tamalpais region has been set aside as a wildlife preserve along one of California's most beautiful coastal regions, one can roam at will with only such limitations as are necessary to insure the preservation of plant and animal life. It is no wonder that this is a favorite spot for hikers, picnickers, and nature enthusiasts. The area's coastland trails skirt the Pacific, revealing sudden glimpses of sea and cliff. These footpaths wind among redwoods, laurels, and madrones; they follow upland streams and circle lakes and lagoons that shimmer in the sunlight. Other trails follow deep ravines that are surrounded by stately trees and blanketed with numerous varieties of ferns.

In the spring, Mount Tamalpais' steep hills are green with fresh grass, and one can see patches of yellow and blue wildflowers. In the summer, white fog often streaks the skyline for miles, and from the summit the upper surface of the fog seen in brilliant sunlight gives the impression of otherworldliness—constantly changing and always unique.

San Francisco Bay, the Pacific Ocean, and miles of hills lie at the viewer's feet.

Madron Grove

A mountain wilderness set aside in its primitive state

Point Reyes

Thrusting its granite headlands twenty miles into the Pacific, Point Reyes is one of the last great natural seashore areas. This triangular peninsula, which is still unspoiled, lies just fifty miles north of San Francisco.

Point Reyes is slowly becoming separated from the mainland as a result of movement along the San Andreas Fault. It was here at Point Reyes that the greatest movement of earth occurred during the catastrophic 1906 earthquake, which devastated the city of San Francisco and thrust the entire peninsula of Point Reyes twenty feet northward into the sea. Today, the movement continues at the rate of two inches per year, and it is the opinion of many geologists that eventually the peninsula will break off completely and become an island.

Awesome and yet appealing to the adventurous, Point Reyes reaches out to meet the Pacific and exposes itself to the full force of the sea. According to official weather records, Point Reyes is the windiest and foggiest spot on the California coast; at times, the winds are so intense that people actually have difficulty standing.

The diversity and beauty of Point Reyes overshadows its severe weather and provides visitors with the same view as the one that greeted Sir Francis Drake when he arrived here four centuries ago.* Upon sailing into the great bay, Drake was met with scenes that have changed little since then—forest-covered ridges, fresh-water lakes, rolling sand dunes, wind-carved islands, and tall white cliffs.

After Drake and his men had plundered the New World settlements along the coast, they hid from pursuing Spanish galleons in the shelter of the bay; here they marveled at the white-faced bluffs fringing the bay in an immense, crescent-shaped sweep that was reminiscent of the white cliffs of Dover.

For six weeks, Drake and his men remained, reconditioning their ship and causing wonderment among the awe-struck Native Americans who inhabited the area. Drake traveled inland with his men, leaving behind a brass plate claiming the land for the Queen of England. But the party must not have traveled far since no mention of the redwoods is made in accounts of the voyage. Their failure to discover San Francisco Bay is due to the fact that they did not scale Mount Tamalpais, although they must have passed the entrance in a mist or fog. It remained for the Spanish explorers to discover the great bay and the giant trees two centuries later.

Although most historians agree that Drake landed at Point Reyes, a few still have doubts. Drake's account is taken from records kept by members of his crew.

High cliffs surround Drake's Bay.

A forested ridge along the foggiest point in California

A mountain of shells greets visitors at Jensen's Oyster Beds.

Dock fishing at Bodega Bay

Coastline at Sonoma Coast State Beach

Fort Ross

Once a chief outpost of Russian civilization in California, Fort Ross stands on a high shelf sloping from wooded hills to the edge of the Pacific. In 1812, the Russians found the rocky inlet above Bodega Bay, gave the local Native Americans some beads in exchange for a thousand acres, and set to building a log fort, which they called *Ross*, the ancient term for Russia.

In quest of food for the starving Russian settlement at Sitka, Alaska, the Russians had planned to establish additional settlements as sources of food supply for its fur-trading posts in the north.

At Fort Ross, the Russians built a stockade using redwood poles to enclose a rectangular area with blockhouses containing cannons in two corners and their Greek Orthodox chapel in another. Within the stockade stood the commandant's house, barracks, warehouses, and a jail; outside were many workshops and crude dwellings, making a total of 59 buildings in all.

The inhabitants of Fort Ross hunted sea otters for pelts, engaged in a few

lines of manufacturing, and grew crops, including sloeberries to flavor vodka. Despite the efforts of apprehensive Spanish officials to check the growth at Fort Ross, the colonists began a thriving trade. The Russian settlement had become a stronger outpost than the Spanish presidios in San Francisco, and the Spanish and Mexican authorities worried about the prospect of Russia taking over all of northern California.

The Russians issued an imperial order forbidding access to the North Pacific to all but Russian ships. Alarmed by this move, President James Monroe countered with his famous Monroe Doctrine of 1823. Foreign insurgents were ordered off the continent. However, Washington was far away and at that time of little consequence. California was now open to Russian conquest.

But the Russians eventually ran into economic difficulties. Years of overkilling had almost exterminated the otter herds, gophers had begun to eat the crops, and there was trouble in the homeland. After thirty-nine years, the once-thriving settlement was to end in failure. The Czar ordered the withdrawal of his subjects, and the fort was sold to John Sutter.

Sutter dismantled the buildings at Fort Ross and shipped everything he could to Sutter's Mill (Sacramento). The transferred property included livestock, industrial machinery, and an arsenal with cannons and muskets—all French weapons picked up in 1813 in the path of Napoleon's historic retreat through the snows of Moscow. The fort and outbuildings eventually fell into ruin, partly as a result of the earthquake of 1906.

Russian Chapel

The road is narrow and winding as it climbs the mountain ledges.

Clusters of rock formations, with their striking earth tones, are a common sight along the northern coastline.

Reminders of an earlier generation

Tangled cypress windbreak

Endless miles of zig-zag split-rail fence

Mendocino

A village of Victorian buildings clustered together on a windswept headland in northern California, Mendocino lies on the northern shore of a crescent-shaped bay at the mouth of Big River. Resembling a Cape Cod hamlet, it is a settlement of steepled churches, water towers, false-front stores, and gabled houses—all with a weatherworn air about them.

The architecture of Mendocino's buildings reflects the New England origin of most of its early settlers. At first glance, the town appears to have scarcely changed since the 1800s. There is the Masonic Hall with the statue of Father Time and the Maiden on the top, the Presbyterian Church, Oddfellows Hall, the Mendocino Hotel, and the cherished old houses.

The homes and buildings in Mendocino have been variously classified as gothic, saltbox, revival, rustic, and even gingerbread. Careful community planning encouraged family use and comfort but also allowed for the picturesque arrange-

ments and charming exteriors, which are still predominant.

New settlers had been lured to California by the Gold Rush of 1849. While most of them had a fling at mining, only those lucky enough to "strike it rich" continued to mine. Others were looking for something more permanent. They wanted to bring their families out to this new land and settle down. Some of these men knew lumbering from their old homes in Maine, New Hampshire, Connecticut, and Vermont. They were strong, courageous people who wanted to sink their roots and stay put. They found their opportunity in 1852 when Henry Meiggs built a sawmill at Mendocino and began supplying lumber to the booming town of San Francisco to the south.

And so a town was born and grew into a thriving lumber community. The lumbermen harvested the trees growing by the sea until the original feverish demand for redwood diminished. When the boom finally came to an end, the mills closed, many of the town's inhabitants left, and Mendocino slept. Those unable to move on remained in Mendocino throughout the depressed years until, many years later, the town was rediscovered, this time by the artists. The artists refurbished old buildings and moved their studios and galleries here. The Mendocino Art Center, which was built on the site of an old mansion, continues to attract amateur painters as well as artists of international renown to the village. Today residents and visitors alike enjoy strolling along the town's wooden sidewalks and visiting its many galleries.

Presbyterian Church built in 1868

Located on an isolated northern California headland, the Victorian town of Mendocino seems to resist change.

Russian Gulch

Although the name suggests that Russians once inhabited this region, no record exists to verify this assumption. It is known that there was once a lumber mill here and a little village, and that during prohibition smuggling and rum running occurred along the shoreline. But now the park, with its tree-lined creek and rocky coast, enjoys a peaceful solitude.

Russian Gulch State Park offers both the serenity of stately redwood groves and the excitement of the turbulent Pacific; it includes a gentle, sandy beach and a high, rocky headland. Sea arches and interesting offshore rock formations, such as a small island with wind-blown trees, amplify the beauty of the rugged cliffs. The beach is suitable for sunbathing and swimming, although the water is cold. It is also used as an entry point for skin-divers who want to explore nearby underwater areas or hunt for abalone and other seafood delicacies.

Continuing inland from the coast, the park extends for nearly three miles into the heavily forested Russian Gulch Creek

Canyon. The visitor can take advantage of picnic sites on the headland and near the beach as well as campsites in the protected canyon. A scenic drive affords easy vantage points of the lower part of the fern-banked canyon, and for more adventurous visitors, a hiking trail continues inland past a beautiful waterfall. Enhanced by the deep-shaded canyon and sparkling sunlight, the waterfall is a splendid sight and a lovely place to relax amidst unspoiled natural beauty.

The canyon is filled with second-growth redwood, Douglas fir, western hemlock, tanoak, and California laurel. Alders and big-leaf maples can be found along the creek. Inside this forest, there are rhododendrons, azaleas, many kinds of ferns, and thimbleberry, salmonberry, and blackberry bushes. Bishop pine, Mendocino cypress, and coast live oaks grow higher up on the slopes.

The prevailing winds along the headland have carved and twisted many of the trees into fascinating shapes, and a sea-cut tunnel called the Devil's Punch Bowl provides a spectacular point of interest. This bowl, which is about 200 feet long, has collapsed at its inland end making a hole 100 feet across and 60 feet deep. The walls of the bowl are steep and lined with clusters of wildflowers, and the water at its bottom moves continuously under the influence of the restless surf. This is one of the many "blow-holes" along the Mendocino coast, but though waves can be seen coming in through the tunnel, the bowl is too broad and open for any "blowing" effect to be noticeable except in particularly stormy weather.

Wooded island at the mouth of Russian Gulch Canyon

The interior of lush, fern-banked Russian Gulch Canyon

Russian Gulch Falls

This narrow harbor lies at the mouth of placid, winding Noyo River, where small fishing craft crowd the area alongside the old warehouses.

North Coast Redwoods

Unique to California, the coast redwood (*Sequoia sempervirens*) is closely related to the Sierra redwood, except that the latter is thicker in girth and does not attain the height of the sempervirens. The coast redwood belt is about 500 miles long and varies in width from one to 30 miles inland. The belt extends from Big Sur's Santa Lucia Mountains in the south all the way to the Oregon border. The main part of the belt and the most impressive groves are located in parks along the famous Redwood Highway (U.S. 101) north of Leggett.

The coast redwood is definitely the tallest of living things, with some trees reaching heights of over 360 feet. But no set of statistics can begin to describe the beauty, grandeur, and majestic serenity of these trees, especially where they grow best—in dense groves alongside the various streams of coastal northern California. The great beauty of these groves results in part from the dramatic contrast they present: the rough-textured red bark of the massive, yet graceful, soaring trunks; the delicate greenery of redwood foliage; the lush carpet of moss and fern on the forest floor; the sunlight

moving slowly over these colors and textures in ever-changing patterns. Along with this, there is the special silence of a redwood grove—the silence of peace and strength, of beings living at ease with their past and secure in their future.

Humboldt Redwood State Park has a magnificent forest of coast redwoods that is being carefully and thoughtfully preserved for the appreciation and enjoyment of the people. Here, amid 2,000-year-old trees, in a forest that began more than 20 million years ago, one can sense the long, slow, joyous procession of life on earth.

Following the south fork of the Eel River, the 33-mile-long Avenue of the Giants traverses the park. This world-renown parkway passes through a giant forest where the air is cool and fragrant and long beams of sunlight slant down through the redwood foliage.

The highlight of the park, and perhaps the finest grove of coast redwoods in California, is the Rockefeller Forest along Bull Creek. It is the most valuable tract of timber in the world and boasts many trees over 360 feet high as well as a number of natural oddities.

Patrick's Point State Park is a tree-and-meadow-covered headland with a broad sandy beach that juts into the Pacific Ocean. The park is characterized by heavy stands of alder and spruce timber interspersed with open meadows which produce a showy display of wildflowers in the spring. On Agate Beach, driving winds and the high tides of winter cause the sea to deposit semiprecious stones on the beach where they are washed and polished by the constant motion of sand and water.

Prairie Creek Redwoods State Park's tall redwood trees grow along the edge of a bluff high above a wild, sandy beach. Fern Canyon, a natural canyon cut through the bluffs by Home Creek, is one of the park's major attractions. Five-fingered ferns grow profusely and thickly cover the canyon's 50-foot-high walls. Prairie Creek is also noted for its two herds of Roosevelt elk, which are the largest deer in North America, with the exception of the moose. Mature bull elk sometimes reach 1,000 pounds and although these animals may appear tame and friendly, it should be remembered that they are wild creatures and can be dangerous.

Del Norte Coast Redwoods State Park lies in the heart of California's rain forest country. Here, an average annual rainfall of 80 inches and a temperate, foggy climate foster tree and plant growth year-round. Many of the most interesting features of the park can be seen from the trails. An outstanding attraction for visitors is the Damnation Creek Trail, which drops steeply through dense, virgin redwood forest to a small beach where tidepools offer the opportunity to study small marine animals.

Jedediah Smith Redwoods State Park lies at the confluence of the Smith River and Mill Creek, less than twelve miles northeast of Crescent City. Its highly attractive setting includes white, fast-running water with many deep pools and primeval forests with lush undergrowth. In contrast to the cool, damp, fogbound summers along the coast, this park's summers are warm and sunny.

Stately redwoods line the banks of the Eel River.

Redwood burls, which are abnormal growths, often form interesting shapes.

Giant redwoods reaching skyward for sunlight

*Ferns carpet the forest floor and decorate
a fallen giant in Rockefeller Forest.*

Lush green beauty along Bull Creek Trail

Redwood stand growing alongside Bull Creek

A small coastal park, Trinidad is dominated by the spectacular Pewetole Island.

Agate Beach, where winter storms and high
tides deposit polished semiprecious stones

Sun-tinted stalks silhouetted against the late afternoon sky

Wild, untamed Gold Bluffs Beach, where redwood growth reaches the Pacific's edge

Magnificent Roosevelt elk can be seen grazing in open areas near the forest's edge.

The bull elk reach 1,000 pounds, and although they appear tame they are actually wild and dangerous.

Babbling Home Creek flows through Fern Canyon,
where five-fingered ferns thrive on the canyon's
moist walls.

One of the finest campsites in California at Red Alder Campground

Among the many species of animals at Del Norte Redwoods are black-tailed deer, bobcat, fox, and black bear.

Damnation Creek Trail winds through dense forest with high redwoods everywhere.

At the end of Damnation Creek Trail is a small, rocky beach covered with driftwood.

At the ocean's edge, on the small beach at the end of Damnation Creek Trail, tidepools offer visitors an opportunity to study marine animals.

Redwoods along Old Stage Coach Road that travels through Jedediah Smith Park. Smith, referred to as a bible toter, was the first white man to cross the Rocky Mountains to the Pacific Coast.

Redwood forests are constantly changing color, depending on the climatic conditions. The colors are never the same but are always superb.

Sparkling view of the Pacific in northern California

California's northernmost edge where the wind seems endless